# A PENGUIN CHICK GROWS UP

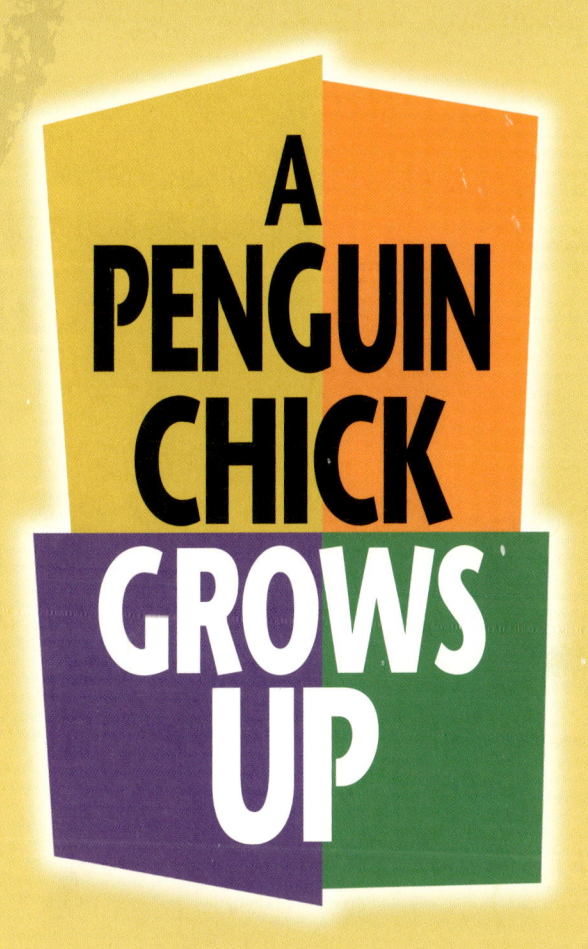

by Joan Hewett
photographs by Richard Hewett

Carolrhoda Books, Inc. / Minneapolis

# Nesting Time on Tuxedo Island

Penguins live on Tuxedo Island.
They make their nests in tunnels.
They line them with grass and twigs.

Mother penguins lay their eggs.
The zookeeper checks the eggs every day.
After 36 days, she hears…
Peep! Peep!

In 2 more days, Obie hatches.
He's a penguin chick.

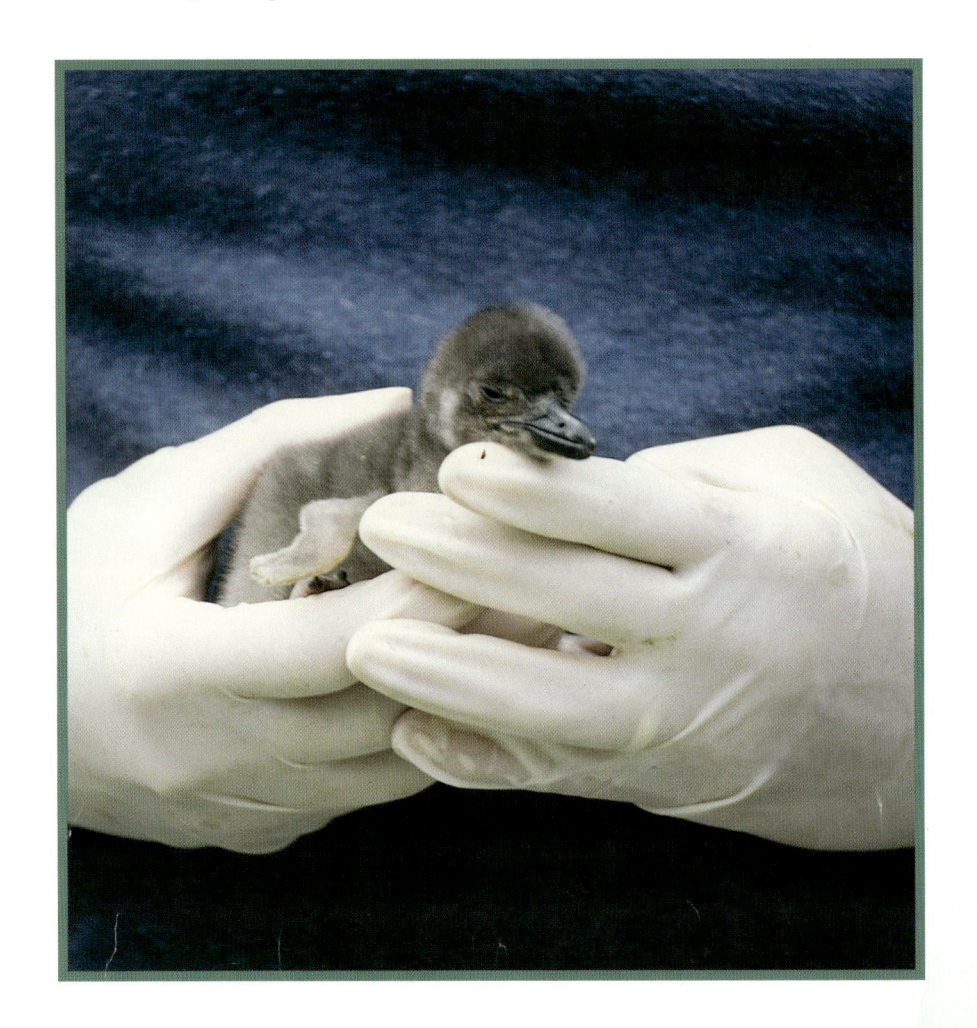

Obie's eyes are still closed.
But the tiny chick is awake.

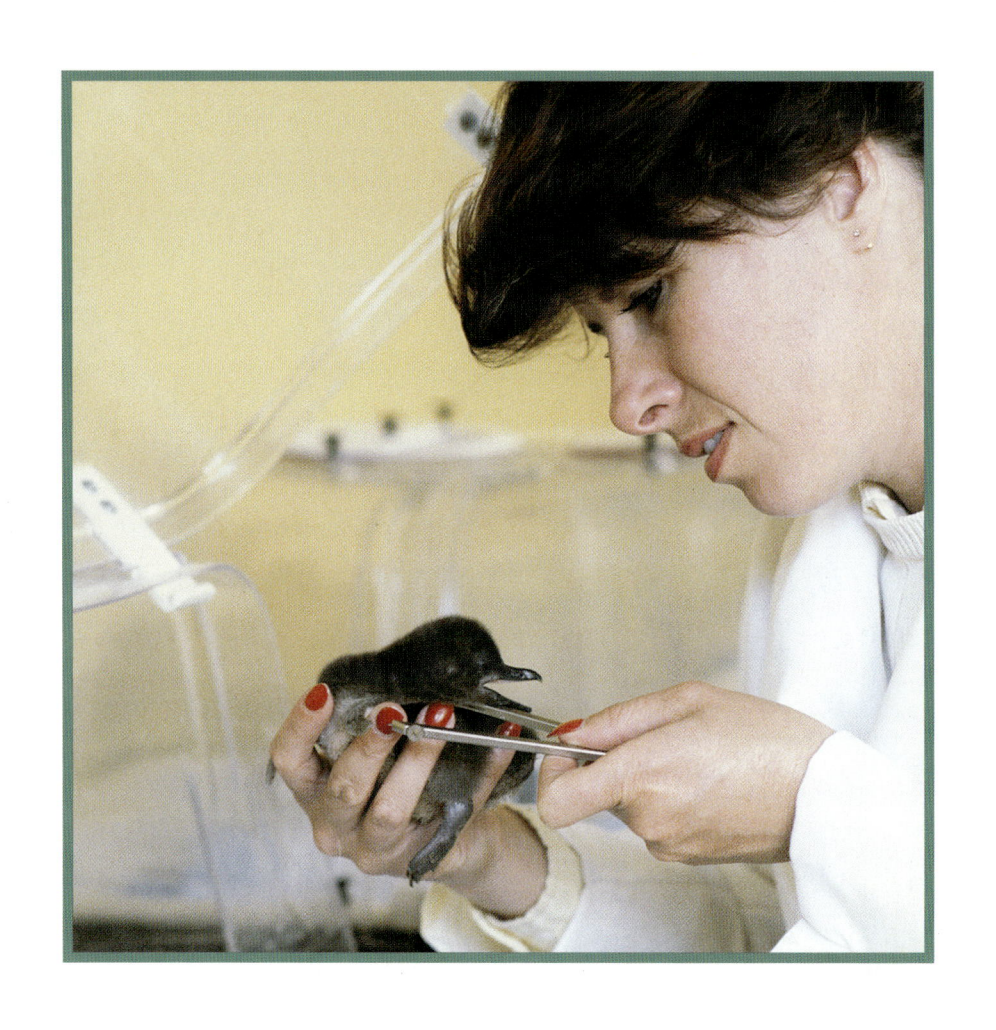

Obie seems like a perfect chick.
The keeper measures him.
He cheeps.

She weighs Obie.

He cheeps again.

The keeper puts him back in his nest.

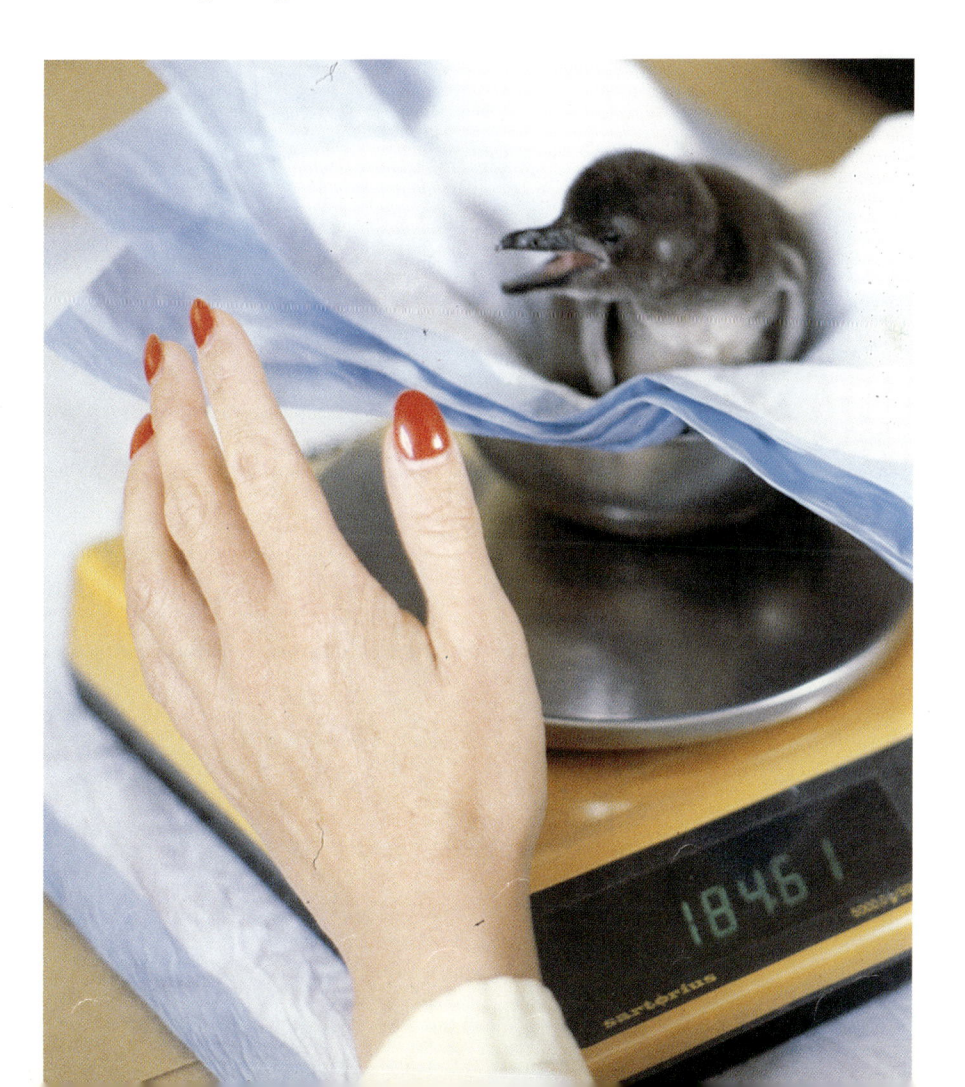

Obie is 3 days old.
The fluffy chick is growing.
His eyes are beginning to open.

The keeper puts a band on his wing.
The band is Obie's nametag.

The keeper returns Obie
to his parents.
They are glad to see him.
The keeper feeds Obie's
father a fish.

Obie's father starts to digest the fish.
Then he coughs it up.
He feeds it to Obie.

# Learning to Walk

By 2 weeks, Obie is chubby.
He no longer fits inside a keeper's hand.

The penguin chicks are curious.
They watch the keepers.
But they barely look at each other.

Obie is 4 weeks old.
He is growing stronger.
His webbed feet are heavy.
But he can shuffle them.

How brave is Obie?

He shuffles to the edge of the tunnel.

He looks out.

Then one day, he goes outside.

Obie's parents stay by his side.
They watch over him and keep him safe.
They clean his coat of feathers.

Obie cheeps.

He is hungry.

His parents feed him.

Obie's coat keeps him warm.
But it doesn't keep him dry.

By 5 weeks, he begins to get new feathers.
They will keep him dry.
They grow in first on the lower part of his body.
Obie seems to be wearing a funny, furry cape.

# LEARNING TO SWIM

Keepers take the chicks from their nests.
They bring them to the bird center.
They will live there for 2 months.

It's time to go swimming.

Penguin chicks don't like to get wet.

They stay away from the water.

A keeper carries Obie into the water.

22

Obie is angry.

He waddles back to shore.

Splish! Splash!

It takes a few weeks.

Then all the chicks are swimming.

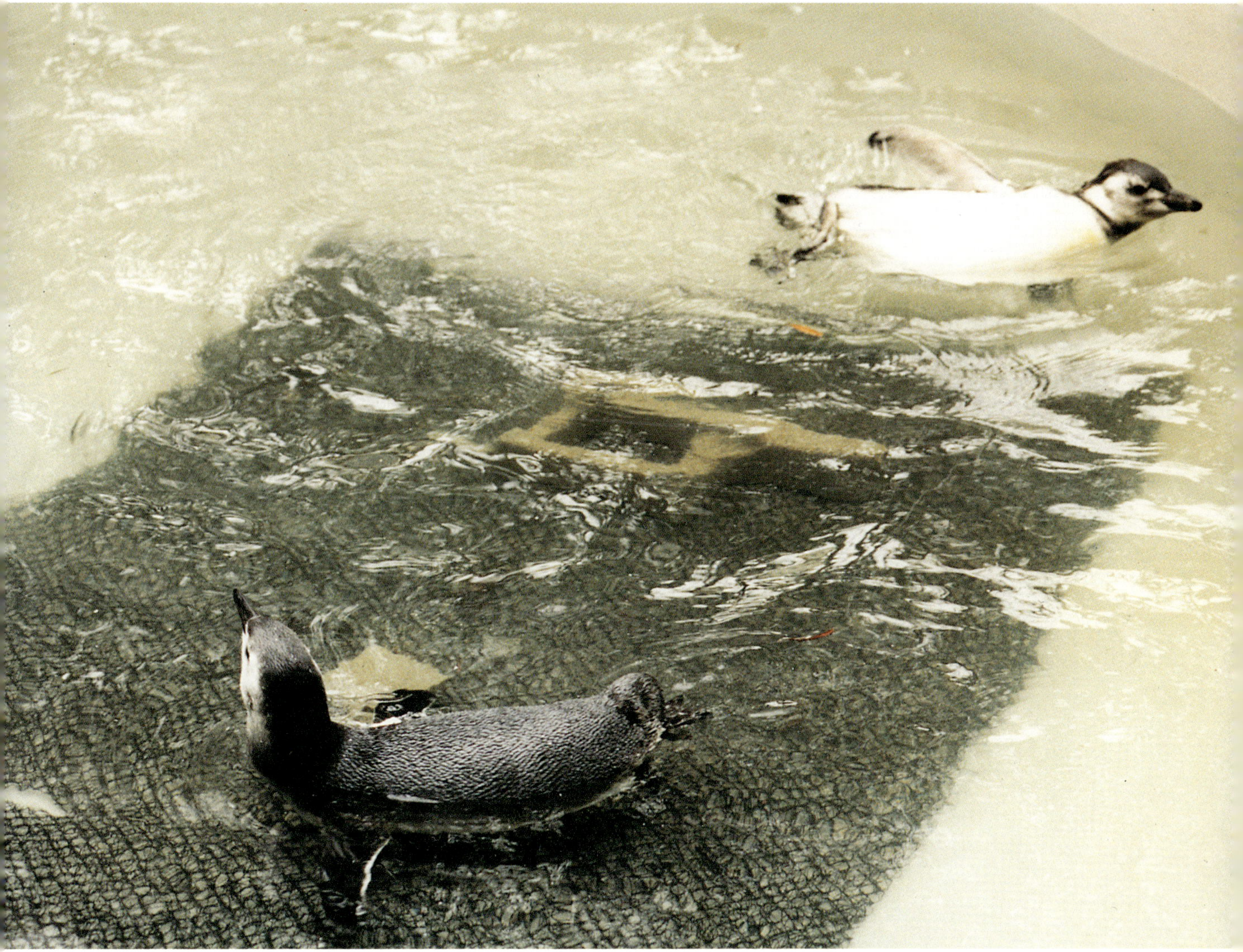

Twice a day, a keeper feeds the chicks.
At first Obie won't eat a whole fish.

Finally he swallows one.
Soon he swallows one fish after another.

Obie takes his last swim at the bird center.
He is ready to go back to Tuxedo Island.

Obie lives with the other young penguins.
In a few years, their adult feathers will grow in.
They will look like they are wearing black-and-white tuxedos.
Obie will be a grown-up.

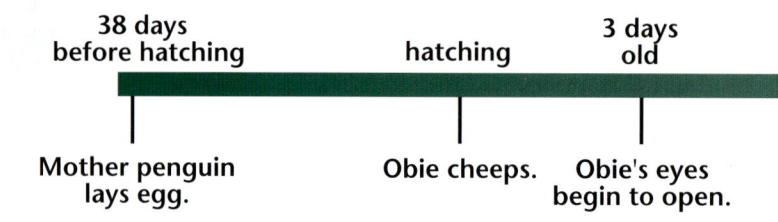

| 38 days before hatching | hatching | 3 days old |
|---|---|---|
| Mother penguin lays egg. | Obie cheeps. | Obie's eyes begin to open. |

### More about Penguins

Penguins are flightless birds. Instead of flying, they swim. Their black and white feathers are coated with oil. The oil keeps the feathers waterproof. Penguins are strong swimmers. They spend most of their lives at sea.

There are 17 species, or kinds, of penguins. Obie is a Magellanic penguin. Magellanic penguins are named for Ferdinand Magellan, an early explorer. Magellanic penguins live in South America. They can be found in the Falkland Islands and in the coastal areas of Chile and Argentina.

When it is time to breed, penguins come ashore. Thousands of Magellanic penguins settle in each rocky seaside colony. Both male and female penguins ready their nests, then feed and care for their helpless chicks.

In the water, penguins are hunted by seals and sea lions. But they are safe from them on land. The birds have no fear of people, so they are easy prey. On land and sea, fishers hunt penguins and penguin eggs for food. Oil tankers often leak oil into the water. The oil coats the penguins' feathers, and often the birds die.

| 4 weeks old | 5 weeks old | | A few years old |
|---|---|---|---|
| Obie can shuffle his feet. | Obie begins to get new feathers. | | Obie is a young adult. |

Can these unique birds continue to thrive in the wild? Chile's Magdalena Island is a national nature reserve. Fishing is banned in the surrounding waters. With plenty of fish and squid, penguins have enough to eat. Oil tankers are also banned, and the water is clean. The well-fed penguins are strong and healthy.

## More about Zoos

Obie and about 50 other Magellanic penguins live at the San Francisco Zoo. Like wild penguins, captive penguins mate for life. Each spring, the birds lay eggs and raise their young.

Zookeepers examine the newborn chicks every day. Magellanic penguins usually have 2 chicks. The larger forceful chick often takes most of the food, while the smaller chick starves. Some penguins lay eggs that don't hatch. A keeper removes those eggs and sets one of the smaller hungry chicks in the nest. The adult penguins accept the chick as their own.

# INDEX

eating, 10–11, 26–27, 29

feathers, 16, 18–19, 29

hatching, 3–4, 31

parents, 2, 10–11, 16–17

shuffling, 14–15

swimming, 21, 22, 24, 25, 28, 30

zookeepers, 3, 5–7, 9–10, 15, 20, 22, 26, 31

For our grandsons, Orson Ridgely, Jesse Angelo, and Nathan Morris

Text copyright © 2004 by Joan Hewett

Photographs copyright © 2004 by Richard R. Hewett
Additional photographs courtesy of Jan Nichols, cover, pp. 21, 22, 23, 24, 25, 26, 27, 28.

All rights reserved. International copyright secured. No part of this book may be reproduced, stored in a retrieval system, or transmitted in any form or by any means—electronic, mechanical, photocopying, recording, or otherwise—without the prior written permission of Carolrhoda Books, Inc., except for brief quotations in an acknowledged review.

This book is available in two editions:
Library binding by Carolrhoda Books, Inc., a division of Lerner Publishing Group
Soft cover by First Avenue Editions, an imprint of Lerner Publishing Group
241 First Avenue North
Minneapolis, MN 55401 U.S.A.

Website address: www.lernerbooks.com

Library of Congress Cataloging-in-Publication Data

Hewett, Joan.
   A penguin chick grows up / by Joan Hewett ; photographs by Richard Hewett.
     p.   cm. — (Baby animals)
   Summary: Describes the development of Obie, a penguin living in a nature sanctuary, from the day he hatches to age five weeks.
   ISBN: 1–57505–200–8 (lib. bdg. : alk. paper)
   ISBN: 1–57505–633–X (pbk. : alk. paper)
   1. Penguins—Infancy—Juvenile literature. [1. Penguins. 2. Animals—Infancy.]
I. Hewett, Richard, ill. II. Title. III. Series.
QL696.S473H49 2004
598.47'139—dc22                                      2003011750

Manufactured in the United States of America
1 2 3 4 5 6 – DP – 09 08 07 06 05 04

WITHDRAWN FROM
HERRICK DISTRICT LIBRARY